G000298381

Captain Kathryn Janeway (Kate Mulgrew) charts the unknown reaches of the Delta Quadrant.

Jeffrey Katz

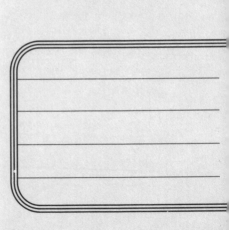

Seven of Nine (Jeri Ryan).

Julie Dennis

STAMP

B'Elanna Torres (Roxann Biggs) tries to construct a beta-tachyon wave generator.

Robbie Robinson

STAMP

Seven of Nine (Jeri Ryan) is captured by the predatory hunters the Hirogen.

Robbie Robinson

STAMP

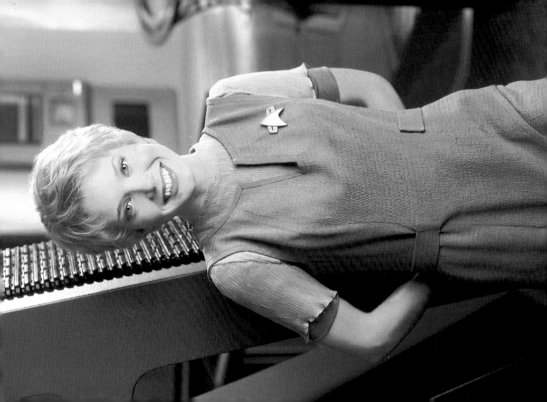

Kes (Jennifer Lien).

Julie Dennis

STAMP

Captain Janeway (Kate Mulgrew) rescues her kidnapped crew members.

Robbie Robinson

STAMP

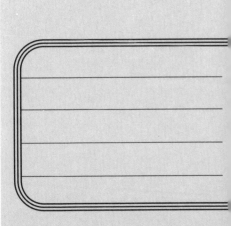

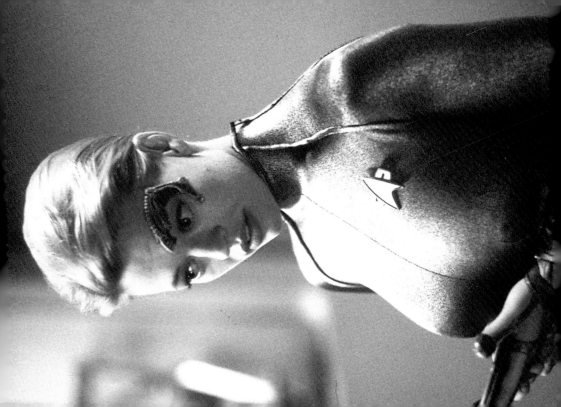

Seven of Nine (Jeri Ryan) studies the designs for a new
Astrometrics lab.

Robbie Robinson

STAMP

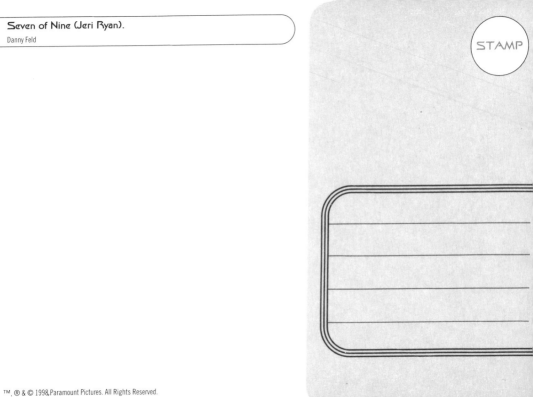

Seven of Nine (Jeri Ryan).

Danny Feld

STAMP

Captain Janeway (Kate Mulgrew) believes she is
Madame Genevieve.

Danny Feld

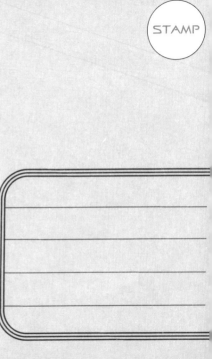

STAMP

Captain Kathryn Janeway (Kate Mulgrew) of the Starship Voyager.

Peter Iovino

STAMP

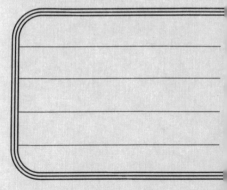

The Ocampan Kes (Jennifer Lien), possessed by an alien dictator's mind.

Robbie Robinson

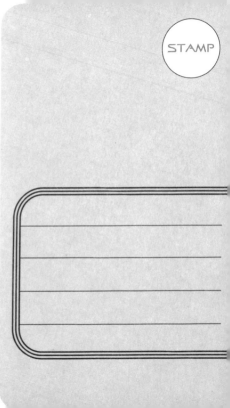

Seven of Nine (Jeri Ryan) remembers her abduction
by the Borg.

Robbie Robinson

STAMP

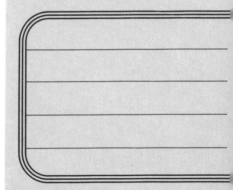

Chief Engineer B'Elanna Torres (Roxann Biggs).

Danny Feld

STAMP

Seven of Nine (Jeri Ryan) believes herself to be a torch singer.

Danny Feld

STAMP

Captain Janeway (Kate Mulgrew) leads the Resistance in a holodeck World War II scenario.

Danny Feld

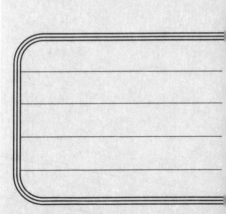

The Borg Drone Seven of Nine, Tertiary Adjunct of Unimatrix Zero One (Jeri Ryan).

Robbie Robinson

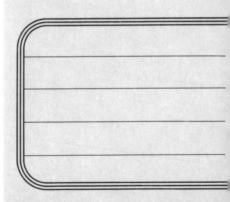

Captain Kathryn Janeway (Kate Mulgrew), commanding officer
of the *Starship Voyager*.

Danny Feld

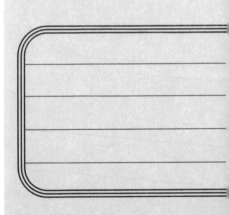

STAMP

Seven of Nine (Jeri Ryan) operates the conn aboard
a shuttlecraft.

Danny Feld

STAMP

B'Elanna Torres (Roxann Biggs) must build a companion for an advanced mechanized intelligence.

Robbie Robinson

STAMP

Kes (Jennifer Lien), Captain Kathryn Janeway (Kate Mulgrew), and Lieutenant B'Elanna Torres (Roxann Biggs).

Julie Dennis

STAMP

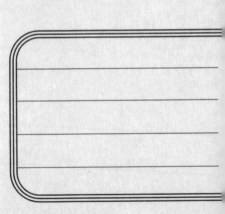

Seven of Nine (Jeri Ryan) sings in a holodeck 1940s club.

Danny Feld

Captain Kathryn Janeway (Kate Mulgrew).

Robbie Robinson

STAMP